The Piano Guys
Uncharted

"Indiana Jones and the Arabian Nights" omitted due to copyright restriction.

ISBN 978-1-4950-7713-5

7777 W. BLUEMOUND RD. P.O. BOX 13819 MILWAUKEE, WI 53213

Visit Hal Leonard Online at
www.halleonard.com

Visit The Piano Guys at
www.thepianoguys.com

As performed by The Piano Guys

FIGHT SONG/AMAZING GRACE

Words and Music by RACHEL PLATTEN
and DAVE BASSETT
Arranged by Al van der Beek,
Steven Sharp Nelson and Jon Schmidt

As performed by The Piano Guys

A SKY FULL OF STARS

Words and Music by GUY BERRYMAN,
JON BUCKLAND, WILL CHAMPION,
CHRIS MARTIN and TIM BERGLING
Arranged by Jon Schmidt
and Steven Sharp Nelson

As performed by The Piano Guys

HELLO/LACRIMOSA

Words and Music by ADELE ADKINS
and GREG KURSTIN
Arranged by Steven Sharp Nelson
and Al van der Beek

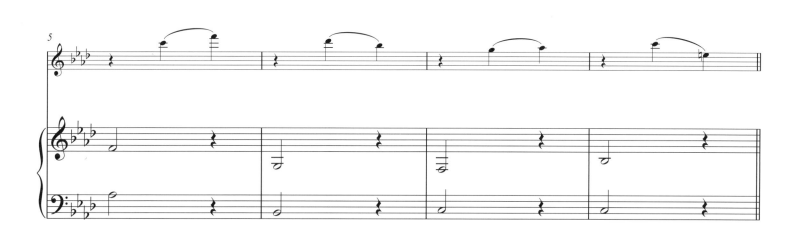

As performed by The Piano Guys

OKAY

Words and Music by ANDY GRAMMER
and DAVE BASSETT
Arranged by Al van der Beek
and Steven Sharp Nelson

but I can't quite drown it out. ___ I'm tor - tured ev - 'ry day. __

These nev - er end - ing wor - ries __ pull - ing at __ my

sleeves. So man - y times now I was s'posed to tap out: all the walls would

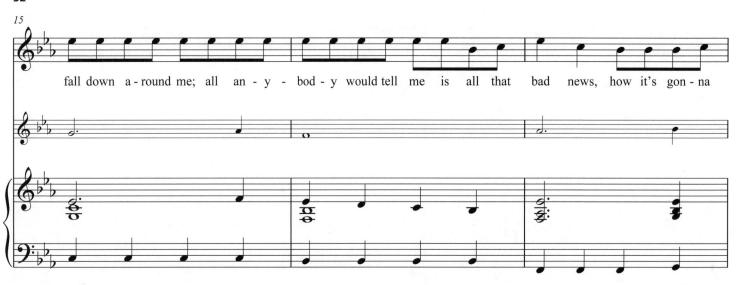

fall down a - round me; all an - y - bod - y would tell me is all that bad news, how it's gon - na

fall through. But no mat - ter what they say, oh, what they ___ say,

it's gon-na be, gon-na be o - kay, ay, ay, ay, ay, ___ ay, ay, ay, ay, _

ay, ay, ay, ay. It's gon-na be, gon-na be o - kay, ay, ay, ay, ay,

ay, ay, ay, ay, ay, ay, ay, ay. No mat - ter what you've

To Coda ⊕

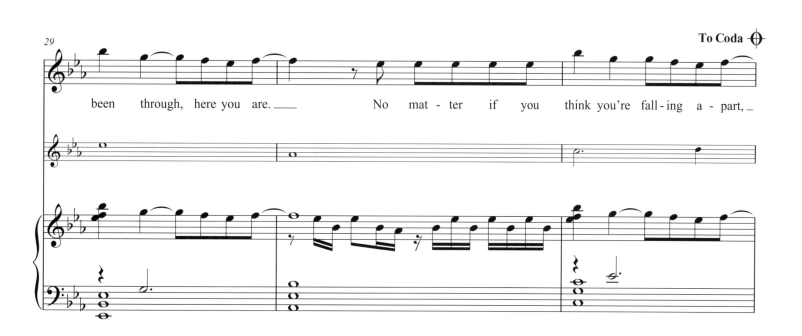

been through, here you are. No mat - ter if you think you're fall-ing a - part,

it's gon-na be o - kay.

And there is a bat-tle rag-ing in ___ your heart, but you ___ must win. ___ It comes for all of us, ___

say-ing we are not e - nough. __ So fight for your life: __ the world's gon-na try __

to sell you some lies. __ So man - y times now I was s'posed to

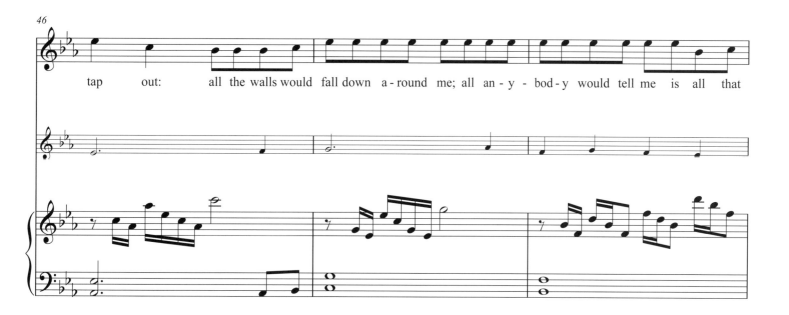

tap out: all the walls would fall down a - round me; all an - y - bod - y would tell me is all that

bad news, how it's gon - na fall through. But no mat - ter what they say, oh, what they _ say,

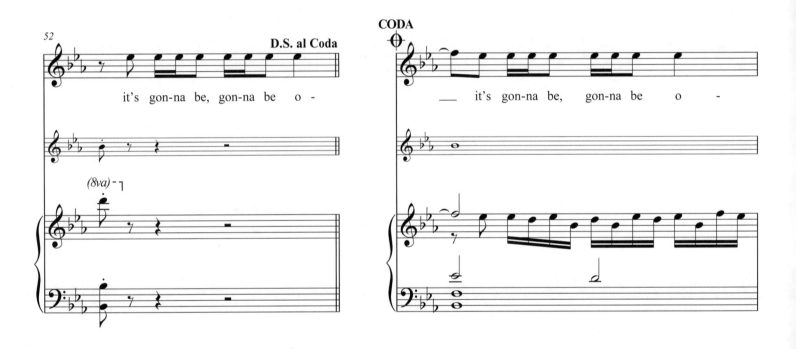

D.S. al Coda

it's gon-na be, gon-na be o -

CODA

_ it's gon-na be, gon-na be o -

kay, ay, ay, ay, ay, ___ ay, ay, ay, ay, ___ ay, ay, ay, ay. ___

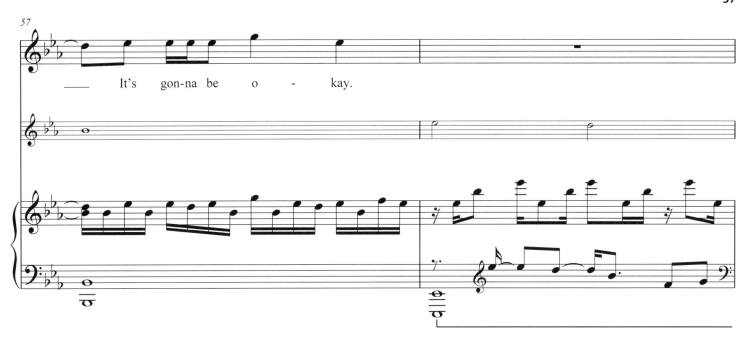

It's gon-na be o - kay.

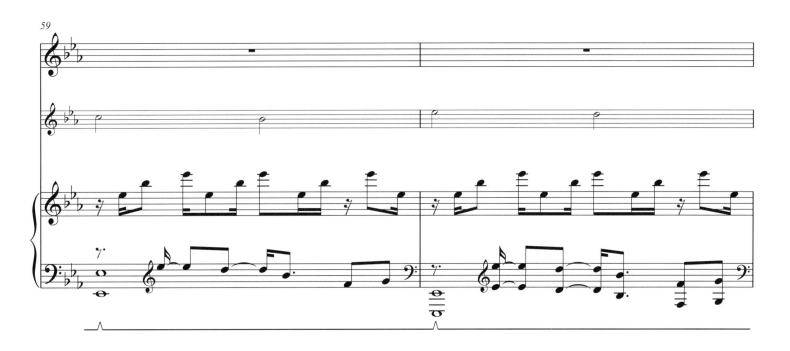

As performed by The Piano Guys

THEMES FROM
PIRATES OF THE CARIBBEAN

Arranged by Gavin Greenaway

Moderately fast, in 4
HE'S A PIRATE
from Walt Disney Pictures' PIRATES OF THE CARIBBEAN: THE CURSE OF THE BLACK PEARL
Music by Klaus Badelt

I DON'T THINK NOW'S THE TIME
from Walt Disney Pictures' PIRATES OF THE CARIBBEAN: AT WORLD'S END
Music by Hans Zimmer

48

THE BLACK PEARL
from Walt Disney Pictures'
PIRATES OF THE CARIBBEAN: THE CURSE OF THE BLACK PEARL
Music by Klaus Badelt

JACK SPARROW
from Walt Disney Pictures'
PIRATES OF THE CARIBBEAN: DEAD MAN'S CHEST
Music by Hans Zimmer

UP IS DOWN
from Walt Disney Pictures' PIRATES OF THE CARIBBEAN: AT WORLD'S END
Music by Hans Zimmer

ONE DAY
from Walt Disney Pictures' PIRATES OF THE CARIBBEAN: AT WORLD'S END
Music by Hans Zimmer

HE'S A PIRATE
from Walt Disney Pictures'
PIRATES OF THE CARIBBEAN:
THE CURSE OF THE BLACK PEARL
Music by Klaus Badelt

As performed by The Piano Guys

CELLOOPA

By STEVEN SHARP NELSON
and AL VAN DER BEEK

*cue notes optional

As performed by The Piano Guys

CAN'T STOP THE FEELING
from TROLLS

Words and Music by JUSTIN TIMBERLAKE,
MAX MARTIN and SHELLBACK
Arranged by Al van der Beek,
Steven Sharp Nelson and Jon Schmidt

Keep on danc - ing. Can't stop the feel -

- ing.

pizz.

Can't stop the feel - ing.   Dance, dance,   dance.

Dance,   dance,   dance. Don't   stop   the feel-

Dance, dance, dance. Can't stop the feel-

-ing. _____ Dance, dance, dance.

Keep on danc - ing.

pizz.

As performed by The Piano Guys

THE JUNGLE BOOK/SARABANDE

Arranged by Al van der Beek,
Jon Schmidt and Steven Sharp Nelson

Moderately fast

MY OWN HOME (Jungle Book Theme)
from Walt Disney's THE JUNGLE BOOK
Words and Music by RICHARD M. SHERMAN and ROBERT B. SHERMAN

*Bottom note optional

THE BARE NECESSITIES
from Walt Disney's
THE JUNGLE BOOK
Words and Music by
TERRY GILKYSON

As performed by The Piano Guys

HOLDING ON

By JON SCHMIDT,
AL VAN DER BEEK and STEVEN SHARP NELSON

no pedal lift

half ped. lift

As performed by The Piano Guys

TOUR DE FRANCE

By JON SCHMIDT

L.H. tremolo

As performed by The Piano Guys

UNCHARTED

By AL VAN DER BEEK
and STEVEN SHARP NELSON